January 2006

Dear Rhea,

   Wishing you many
tender moments with
baby Alan!

      Love & Kisses,

      Jayne

THIRSTY BABY

THIRSTY BABY

By Catherine Ann Cullen

Illustrated by David McPhail

LITTLE, BROWN AND COMPANY

New York · An AOL Time Warner Company

With a loving toast to thirsty baby James Finnegan and to my parents,
Mary Roche and Jack Cullen, who were always there to quench our thirsts:
"Nua gach bidh is sean gach dighe"
(May your food be fresh and your drink old.)
—C. A.C.

For all the people at Little, Brown who took such good care of me and my books over the years—
Goodbye, Boston, and good luck.
—D.M.

First Edition

Library of Congress Cataloging-in-Publication Data

Cullen, Catherine Ann.
    Thirsty Baby/by Catherine Ann Cullen; illustrated by David McPhail.
        p. cm.
    Summary: A thirsty baby gets his drink but always wants more.
    ISBN 0-316-16357-0
    [1. Babies—Fiction. 2. Stories in rhyme.] I. McPhail, David M., ill. II. Title.

PZ8.3.C8885 Th 2002
[E]—dc21

                                                                    2002022493

10 9 8 7 6 5 4 3 2 1

TWP

Printed in Singapore

The illustrations for this book were done in watercolor and ink.
The text was set in Berling, and the display type is Eraser Dust.

"I'm thirsty," said the baby, "and I need a drink."
So we gave him a bottle, and what do you think?

He started with a sip, and he finished with a sup,
And the pink plastic bottle, he drank it all up.

"Good boy!" said Daddy, walking in the door,
But the baby said, "I'm thirsty, and I want MORE!"

"I'm thirsty," said the baby, "and I need a drink."
"Bath time!" shouted Mommy, and what do you think?

He started with a sip, and he finished with a sup,

And the blue bubbly bathtub, he drank it all up.

"Good boy," murmured Mommy as she mopped the floor,
But the baby said, "I'm thirsty, and I want MORE!"

"I'm thirsty," said the baby, "and I need a drink."
We were paddling in the pond, and what do you think?

He started with a sip, and he finished with a sup,

And the pond in the park, why, he drank it all up.

"Good boy," said Sister, though she wasn't sure,
But the baby said, "I'm thirsty, and I want MORE!"

"I'm thirsty," said the baby, "and I need a drink."
We were fishing in the river, and what do you think?

He started with a sip, and he finished with a sup,

And the red rolling river, he drank it all up.

"Good boy," giggled Granny, standing on the shore,
But the baby said, "I'm thirsty, and I want MORE!"

"I'm thirsty," said the baby, "and I need a drink."
We were sitting by the sea, and what do you think?

He started with a sip, and he finished with a sup,

And the shining sea of silver, he drank it all up.

"Good grief!" groaned Grandpa. "We need more of this stuff."
But the baby just burped and said, "That's enough!"

"I drank the bottle and the bathtub too,
And the pond and the river and the sea so blue."

"That's enough!" said the baby. "Now it's time to stop."
"That's enough!" said the baby. "Not another drop!"

"That's enough!" said the baby. "That's enough," he said.
"I won't drink another drop . . . until it's time for bed."